Selected Writings of
Bahá'u'lláh

Author of the Bahá'í Dispensation

BAHÁ'Í PUBLISHING COMMITTEE
WILMETTE, ILLINOIS
1942

Prayer for Union in the Law of God

Lauded be Thy name, O Lord my God! Darkness hath fallen upon every land, and the forces of mischief have encompassed all the nations. Through them, however, I perceive the splendors of Thy wisdom, and discern the brightness of the light of Thy providence.

They that are shut out as by a veil from Thee have imagined that they have the power to put out Thy light, and to quench Thy fire, and to still the winds of Thy grace. Nay, and to this Thy might beareth me witness! Had not every tribulation been made the bearer of Thy wisdom, and every ordeal the vehicle of Thy providence, no one would have dared oppose us, though the powers of earth and heaven were to be leagued against us. Were I to unravel the wondrous mysteries of Thy wisdom which are laid bare before me, the reins of Thine enemies would be cleft asunder.

Glorified be Thou, then, O my God! I beseech Thee by Thy Most Great Name to assemble them that love Thee around the Law that streameth from the good-pleasure of Thy will, and to send down upon them what will assure their hearts.

Potent art Thou to do what pleaseth Thee. Thou art, verily, the Help in Peril, the Self-Subsisting.

SELECTED WRITINGS OF
BAHÁ'U'LLÁH
AUTHOR OF THE BAHÁ'Í DISPENSATION

The Ocean of Mercy

1. This is the Day in which God's most excellent favors have been poured out upon men, the Day in which His most mighty grace hath been infused into all created things. It is incumbent upon all the peoples of the world to reconcile their differences, and, with perfect unity and peace, abide beneath the shadow of the Tree of His care and loving-kindness. It behoveth them to cleave to whatsoever will, in this Day, be conducive to the exaltation of their stations, and to the promotion of their best interests. Happy are those whom the all-glorious Pen was moved to remember, and blessed are those men whose names, by virtue of Our inscrutable decree, We have preferred to conceal.

Beseech ye the one true God to grant that all men may be graciously assisted to fulfil that which is acceptable in Our sight. Soon will the present-day order be rolled up, and a new one spread out in its stead. Verily, thy Lord speaketh the truth, and is the Knower of things unseen.

2. Say: O men! This is a matchless Day. Matchless must, likewise, be the tongue that celebrateth the praise of the Desire of all nations, and matchless the deed that aspireth to be acceptable in His sight. The whole human race hath longed for this Day, that perchance it may fulfil that which well beseemeth its station, and is worthy of its destiny.

Blessed is the man whom the affairs of the world have failed to deter from recognizing Him Who is the Lord of all things.

So blind hath become the human heart that neither the disruption of the city, nor the reduction of the mountain in dust, nor even the cleaving of the earth, can shake off its torpor. The allusions made in the Scriptures have been unfolded, and the signs recorded therein have been revealed, and the prophetic cry is continually being raised. And yet all, except such as God was pleased to guide, are bewildered in the drunkenness of their heedlessness!

Witness how the world is being afflicted with a fresh calamity every day. Its tribulation is continually deepening. From the moment the Súriy-i-Ra'ís (Tablet to Ra'ís) was revealed until the present day, neither hath the world been tranquillized, nor have the hearts of its peoples been at rest. At one time it hath been agitated by contentions and disputes, at another it hath been convulsed by wars, and fallen a victim to inveterate diseases. Its sickness is approaching the stage of utter hopelessness, inasmuch as the true Physician is debarred from administering the remedy, whilst unskilled practitioners are regarded with favor, and are accorded full freedom to act. . . . The dust of sedition hath clouded the hearts of men, and blinded their eyes. Erelong, they will perceive the consequences of what their hands have wrought in the Day of God. Thus warneth you He Who is the All-Informed, as bidden by One Who is the Most Powerful, the Almighty.

3. This is the Day whereon the Ocean of God's mercy hath been manifested unto men, the Day in which the Day Star of His loving-kindness hath shed its radiance upon them, the Day in which the clouds of His bountiful favor have overshadowed the whole of mankind. Now is the time to

cheer and refresh the down-cast through the invigorating breeze of love and fellowship, and the living waters of friendliness and charity.

They who are the beloved of God, in whatever place they gather and whomsoever they may meet, must evince, in their attitude towards God, and in the manner of their celebration of His praise and glory, such humility and submissiveness that every atom of the dust beneath their feet may attest the depth of their devotion. The conversation carried by these holy souls should be informed with such power that these same atoms of dust will be thrilled by its influence. They should conduct themselves in such manner that the earth upon which they tread may never be allowed to address to them such words as these: "I am to be preferred above you. For witness, how patient I am in bearing the burden which the husbandman layeth upon me. I am the instrument that continually imparteth unto all beings the blessings with which He Who is the Source of all grace hath entrusted me. Notwithstanding the honor conferred upon me, and the unnumbered evidences of my wealth—a wealth that supplieth the needs of all creation—behold the measure of my humility, witness with what absolute submissiveness I allow myself to be trodden beneath the feet of men. . . ."

Show forbearance and benevolence and love to one another. Should any one among you be incapable of grasping a certain truth, or be striving to comprehend it, show forth, when conversing with him, a spirit of extreme kindliness and good-will. Help him to see and recognize the truth, without esteeming yourself to be, in the least, superior to him, or to be possessed of greater endowments.

The whole duty of man in this Day is to attain that share of the flood of grace which God poureth forth for him. Let none, therefore, consider the largeness or smallness of the receptacle. The portion of some might lie in the palm of a man's hand, the portion of others might fill a cup, and of others even a gallon-measure.

God and His Manifestations

4. All-praise to the unity of God, and all-honor to Him, the sovereign Lord, the incomparable and all-glorious Ruler of the universe, Who, out of utter nothingness, hath created the reality of all things, Who, from naught, hath brought into being the most refined and subtle elements of His creation, and Who, rescuing His creatures from the abasement of remoteness and the perils of ultimate extinction, hath received them into His kingdom of incorruptible glory. Nothing short of His all-encompassing grace, His all-pervading mercy, could have possibly achieved it. How could it, otherwise, have been possible for sheer nothingness to have acquired by itself the worthiness and capacity to emerge from its state of non-existence into the realm of being?

Having created the world and all that liveth and moveth therein, He, through the direct operation of His unconstrained and sovereign Will, chose to confer upon man the unique distinction and capacity to know Him and to love Him—a capacity that must needs be regarded as the generating impulse and the primary purpose underlying the whole of creation. . . . Upon the inmost reality of each and every created thing He hath shed the light of one of His attributes. Upon the reality of man, however, He hath focused the radiance of all of His names and attributes, and made it a mirror of His own Self. Alone of all created things man hath been singled out for so great a favor, so enduring a bounty.

These energies with which the Day Star of Divine bounty and Source of heavenly guidance hath endowed the reality of man lie, however, latent within him, even as the flame is hidden within the candle and the rays of light are potentially present in the lamp. The radiance of these energies may be obscured by worldly desires even as the light of the sun can be concealed beneath the dust and dross which cover the mirror. Neither the candle nor the lamp can be lighted through their own unaided efforts, nor can it ever be possible for the mirror to free itself from its dross. It is clear and evident that until a fire is kindled the lamp will never be ignited, and unless the dross is blotted out from the face of the mirror it can never represent the image of the sun nor reflect its light and glory.

And since there can be no tie of direct intercourse to bind the one true God with His creation, and no resemblance whatever can exist between the transient and the Eternal, the contingent and the Absolute, He hath ordained that in every age and dispensation a pure and stainless Soul be made manifest in the kingdoms of earth and heaven. Unto this subtle, this mysterious and ethereal Being He hath assigned a twofold nature; the physical, pertaining to the world of matter, and the spiritual, which is born of the substance of God Himself.

5. To every discerning and illuminated heart it is evident that God, the unknowable Essence, the Divine Being, is immensely exalted beyond every human attribute, such as corporeal existence, ascent and decent, egress and regress. Far be it from His glory that human tongue should adequately recount His praise, or that human heart comprehend His fathomless mystery. He is, and hath ever been, veiled in the ancient eternity of His Essence, and will remain in His Reality everlastingly hidden from the sight of men. "No vision taketh in Him, but He taketh in all vision; He is the Subtile, the All-Perceiving." . . .

9

The door of the knowledge of the Ancient of Days being thus closed in the face of all beings, the Source of infinite grace, according to His saying, "His grace hath transcended all things; My grace hath encompassed them all," hath caused those luminous Gems of Holiness to appear out of the realm of the spirit, in the noble form of the human temple, and be made manifest unto all men, that they may impart unto the world the mysteries of the unchangeable Being, and tell of the subtleties of His imperishable Essence.

These sanctified Mirrors, these Day Springs of ancient glory, are, one and all, the Exponents on earth of Him Who is the central Orb of the universe, its Essence and ultimate Purpose. From Him proceed their knowledge and power; from Him is derived their sovereignty. The beauty of their countenance is but a reflection of His image, and their revelation a sign of His deathless glory. They are the Treasuries of Divine knowledge, and the Repositories of celestial wisdom. Through them is transmitted a grace that is infinite, and by them is revealed the Light that can never fade. . . . These Tabernacles of Holiness, these Primal Mirrors which reflect the light of unfading glory, are but expressions of Him Who is the Invisible of the Invisibles. By the revelation of these Gems of Divine virtue all the names and attributes of God, such as knowledge and power, sovereignty and dominion, mercy and wisdom, glory, bounty, and grace, are made manifest.

These attributes of God are not, and have never been, vouchsafed specially unto certain Prophets, and withheld from others. Nay, all the Prophets of God, His well-favored, His holy and chosen Messengers are, without exception, the bearers of His names, and the embodiments of His attributes. They only differ in the intensity of their revelation, and the comparative potency of their light. Even as He hath revealed: "Some of the Apostles We have caused to excel the others."

10

It hath, therefore, become manifest and evident that within the tabernacles of these Prophets and chosen Ones of God the light of His infinite names and exalted attributes hath been reflected, even though the light of some of these attributes may or may not be outwardly revealed from these luminous Temples to the eyes of men. That a certain attribute of God hath not been outwardly manifested by these Essences of Detachment doth in no wise imply that they who are the Day Springs of God's attributes and the Treasuries of His holy names did not actually possess it. Therefore, these illuminated Souls, these beauteous Countenances have, each and every one of them, been endowed with all the attributes of God, such as sovereignty, dominion, and the like, even though to outward seeming they be shorn of all earthly majesty. . . .

6. Know thou assuredly that the essence of all the Prophets of God is one and the same. Their unity is absolute. God, the Creator, saith: There is no distinction whatsoever among the Bearers of My Message. They all have but one purpose; their secret is the same secret. To prefer one in honor to another, to exalt certain ones above the rest, is in no wise to be permitted. Every true Prophet hath regarded His Message as fundamentally the same as the Revelation of every other Prophet gone before Him. If any man, therefore, should fail to comprehend this truth, and should consequently indulge in vain and unseemly language, no one whose sight is keen and whose understanding is enlightened would ever allow such idle talk to cause him to waver in his belief.

The measure of the revelation of the Prophets of God in this world, however, must differ. Each and every one of them hath been the Bearer of a distinct Message, and hath been commissioned to reveal Himself through specific acts. It is for this reason that they appear to vary in their greatness. Their Revelation may be likened unto the light of the moon that sheddeth its radiance upon the earth. Though every time it appeareth, it revealeth a fresh measure of its brightness, yet its inherent splendor can never diminish, nor can its light suffer extinction.

It is clear and evident, therefore, that any apparent variation in the intensity of their light is not inherent in the light itself, but should rather be attributed to the varying receptivity of an ever-changing world. Every Prophet Whom the Almighty and Peerless Creator hath purposed to send to the peoples of the earth hath been entrusted with a Message, and charged to act in a manner that would best meet the requirements of the age in which He appeared. God's purpose in sending His Prophets unto men is twofold. The first is to liberate the children of men from the darkness of ignorance, and guide them to the light of true understanding. The second is to insure the peace and tranquillity of mankind, and provide all the means by which they can be established.

The Prophets of God should be regarded as physicians whose task is to foster the well-being of the world and its peoples, that, through the spirit of oneness, they may heal the sickness of a divided humanity. To none is given the right to question their words or disparage their conduct, for they are the only ones who can claim to have understood the patient and to have correctly diagnosed its ailments. No man, however acute his perception, can ever hope to reach the heights which the wisdom and understanding of the Divine Physician have attained. Little wonder, then, if the treatment prescribed by the physician in this day should not be found to be identical with that which he prescribed before. How could it be otherwise when the ills affecting the sufferer necessitate at every stage of his sickness a special remedy? In like manner, every time the Prophets of God have illumined the world with the resplendent radiance of the Day Star of Divine knowledge, they have invariably summoned its peoples to embrace the light of God through such means as best befitted the exigencies of the age in which they appeared. They were thus able to scatter the darkness of ignorance, and to shed upon the world the glory of their own knowledge. It is towards the inmost essence of these Prophets, therefore, that the eye of every man of discernment must be directed, inasmuch as their one and only purpose hath always been to guide the erring, and give peace to the afflicted. These are not days of prosperity and triumph. The whole of mankind is in the grip of manifold ills. Strive, therefore, to save its life through the wholesome medicine which the almighty hand of the unerring Physician hath prepared.

And now concerning thy question regarding the nature of religion. Know thou that they who are truly wise have likened the world unto the human temple. As the body of man needeth a garment to clothe it, so the body of mankind must needs be adorned with the mantle of justice and wisdom. Its robe is the Revelation vouchsafed unto it by God. Whenever this robe hath fulfilled its purpose, the Almighty will assuredly renew it. For every age requireth a fresh measure of the light of God. Every Divine Revelation hath been sent down in a manner that befitted the circumstances of the age in which it hath appeared.

As to thy question regarding the sayings of the leaders of past religions. Every wise and praiseworthy man will no doubt eschew such vain and profitless talk. The incomparable Creator hath created all men from one same substance, and hath exalted their reality above the rest of His creatures. Success or failure, gain or loss, must, therefore, depend upon man's own exertions.

7. Beware, O believers in the Unity of God, lest ye be tempted to make any distinction between any of the Manifestations of His Cause, or to discriminate against the signs that have accompanied and proclaimed their Revelation. This indeed is the true meaning of Divine Unity, if ye be of them that apprehend and believe this truth. Be ye assured, moreover, that the works and acts of each and every one of these Manifestations of God, nay whatever pertaineth unto them, and whatsoever they may manifest in the future, are all ordained by God, and are a reflection of His Will and Purpose. Whoso maketh the slightest possible difference between their persons, their words, their messages, their acts and manners, hath indeed disbelieved in God, hath repudiated His signs, and betrayed the Cause of His Messengers.

8. Know thou that when the Son of Man (Christ) yielded up His breath to God, the whole creation wept with a great weeping. By sacrificing Himself, however, a fresh capacity was infused into all created things. Its evidences, as witnessed in all the peoples of the earth, are now manifest before thee. The deepest wisdom which the sages have uttered, the profoundest learning which any mind hath unfolded, the arts which the ablest hands have produced, the influence exerted by the most potent of rulers, are but manifestations of the quickening power released by His transcendent, His all-pervasive, and resplendent Spirit.

The Path to God

9. How wondrous is the unity of the Living, the Ever-Abiding God—a unity which is exalted above all limitations, that transcendeth the comprehension of all created things! He hath, from everlasting, dwelt in His inacces-

sible habitation of holiness and glory, and will unto ever-lasting continue to be enthroned upon the heights of His independent sovereignty and grandeur. How lofty hath been His incorruptible Essence, how completely independent of the knowledge of all created things, and how immensely exalted will it remain above the praise of all the inhabitants of the heavens and the earth!

From the exalted source, and out of the essence of His favor and bounty, He hath entrusted every created thing with a sign of His knowledge, so that none of His creatures may be deprived of its share in expressing, each according to its capacity and rank, this knowledge. This sign is the mirror of His beauty in the world of creation. The greater the effort exerted for the refinement of this sublime and noble mirror, the more faithfully will it be made to reflect the glory of the names and attributes of God, and reveal the wonders of His signs and knowledge. Every created thing will be enabled (so great is this reflecting power) to reveal the potentialities of its pre-ordained station, will recognize its capacity and limitations, and will testify to the truth that "He, verily, is God; there is none other God besides Him." . . .

10. The vitality of men's belief in God is dying out in every land; nothing short of His wholesome medicine can ever restore it. The corrosion of ungodliness is eating into the vitals of human society; what else but the Elixir of His potent Revelation can cleanse and revive it? Is it within human power, O Ḥakím, to effect in the constituent elements of any of the minute and indivisible particles of matter so complete a transformation as to transmute it into purest gold? Perplexing and difficult as this may appear, the still greater task of converting satanic strength into heavenly power is one that We have been empowered

to accomplish. The Force capable of such a transformation transcendeth the potency of the Elixir itself. The Word of God, alone, can claim the distinction of being endowed with the capacity required for so great and far-reaching a change.

11. The generations that have gone on before you—whither are they fled? And those round whom in life circled the fairest and the loveliest of the land, where now are they? Profit by their example, O people, and be not of them that are gone astray.

Others ere long will lay hands on what ye possess, and enter into your habitations. Incline your ears to My words, and be not numbered among the foolish.

For every one of you his paramount duty is to choose for himself that on which no other may infringe and none usurp from him. Such a thing—and to this the Almighty is My witness—is the love of God, could ye but perceive it.

Build ye for yourselves such houses as the rain and floods can never destroy, which shall protect you from the changes and chances of this life. This is the instruction of Him Whom the world hath wronged and forsaken.

12. That the heart is the throne, in which the Revelation of God the All-Merciful is centered, is attested by the holy utterances which We have formerly revealed. Among them is this saying: "Earth and heaven cannot contain Me; what can alone contain Me is the heart of him that believeth in Me, and is faithful to My Cause." How often hath the human heart, which is the recipient of the light of God and the seat of the revelation of the All-Merciful, erred from Him Who is the Source of that light and the Well Spring of that revelation. It is the waywardness of the heart that

removeth it far from God, and condemneth it to remoteness from Him. Those hearts, however, that are aware of His Presence, are close to Him, and are to be regarded as having drawn nigh unto His throne.

Consider, moreover, how frequently doth man become forgetful of his own self, whilst God remaineth, through His all-encompassing knowledge, aware of His creature, and continueth to shed upon him the manifest radiance of His glory. It is evident, therefore, that, in such circumstances, He is closer to him than his own self. He will, indeed, so remain for ever, for, whereas the one true God knoweth all things, perceiveth all things, and comprehendeth all things, mortal man is prone to err, and is ignorant of the mysteries that lie enfolded within him. . . .

13. Blessed are they that have soared on the wings of detachment and attained the station which, as ordained by God, overshadoweth the entire creation, whom neither the vain imaginations of the learned, nor the multitude of the hosts of the earth have succeeded in deflecting from His Cause. Who is there among you, O people, who will renounce the world, and draw nigh unto God, the Lord of all names? Where is he to be found who, through the power of My name that transcendeth all created things, will cast away the things that men possess, and cling, with all his might, to the things which God, the Knower of the unseen and of the seen, hath bidden him observe? Thus hath His bounty been sent down unto men, His testimony fulfilled, and His proof shone forth above the Horizon of mercy. Rich is the prize that shall be won by him who hath believed and exclaimed: "Lauded art Thou, O Beloved of all worlds! Magnified be Thy name, O Thou the Desire of every understanding heart!"

17

14. Tear asunder, in My Name, the veils that have grievously blinded your vision, and, through the power born of your belief in the unity of God, scatter the idols of vain imitation. Enter, then, the holy paradise of the good-pleasure of the All-Merciful. Sanctify your souls from whatsoever is not of God, and taste ye the sweetness of rest within the pale of His vast and mighty Revelation, and beneath the shadow of His supreme and infallible authority. Suffer not yourselves to be wrapt in the dense veils of your selfish desires, inasmuch as I have perfected in every one of you My creation, so that the excellence of My handiwork may be fully revealed unto men. It follows, therefore, that every man hath been, and will continue to be, able of himself to appreciate the Beauty of God, the Glorified. Had he not been endowed with such a capacity, how could he be called to account for his failure? If, in the Day when all the peoples of the earth will be gathered together, any man should, whilst standing in the presence of God, be asked: "Wherefore hast thou disbelieved in My Beauty and turned away from My Self," and if such a man should reply and say: "Inasmuch as all men have erred, and none hath been found willing to turn his face to the Truth, I, too, following their example, have grievously failed to recognize the Beauty of the Eternal," such a plea will, assuredly, be rejected. For the faith of no man can be conditioned by any one except himself.

15. O My servants! It behoveth you to refresh and revive your souls through the gracious favors which, in this Divine, this soul-stirring Springtime, are being showered upon you. The Day Star of His great glory hath shed its radiance upon you, and the clouds of His limitless grace have overshadowed you. How high the reward of him that hath not

18

deprived himself of so great a bounty, nor failed to recognize the beauty of his Best-Beloved in this, His new attire.

Say: O people! The Lamp of God is burning; take heed, lest the fierce winds of your disobedience extinguish its light. Now is the time to arise and magnify the Lord, your God. Strive not after bodily comforts, and keep your heart pure and stainless. The Evil One is lying in wait, ready to entrap you. Gird yourselves against his wicked devices, and, led by the light of the name of the one true God, deliver yourselves from the darkness that surroundeth you. Center your thoughts in the Well-Beloved, rather than in your own selves.

16. Blessed is the man that hath acknowledged his belief in God and in His signs, and recognized that "He shall not be asked of His doings." Such a recognition hath been made by God the ornament of every belief, and its very foundation. Upon it must depend the acceptance of every goodly deed. Fasten your eyes upon it, that haply the whisperings of the rebellious may not cause you to slip.

Were He to decree as lawful the thing which from time immemorial had been forbidden, and forbid that which had, at all times, been regarded as lawful, to none is given the right to question His authority. Whoso will hesitate, though it be for less than a moment, should be regarded as a transgressor.

Whoso hath not recognized this sublime and fundamental verity, and hath failed to attain this most exalted station, the winds of doubt will agitate him, and the sayings of the infidels will distract his soul. He that hath acknowledged this principle will be endowed with the most perfect constancy.

19

The Paradise of His Presence

17. Release yourselves, O nightingales of God, from the thorns and brambles of wretchedness and misery, and wing your flight to the rose-garden of unfading splendor. O My friends that dwell upon the dust! Haste forth unto your celestial habitation. Announce unto yourselves the joyful tidings: "He Who is the Best-Beloved is come! He hath crowned Himself with the glory of God's Revelation, and hath unlocked to the face of men the doors of His ancient Paradise." Let all eyes rejoice, and let every ear be gladdened, for now is the time to gaze on His beauty, now is the fit time to hearken to His voice. Proclaim unto every longing lover: 'Behold, your Well-Beloved hath come among men!" and to the messengers of the Monarch of love impart the tidings: "Lo, the Adored One hath appeared arrayed in the fullness of His glory!" O lovers of His beauty! Turn the anguish of your separation from Him into the joy of an everlasting reunion, and let the sweetness of His presence dissolve the bitterness of your remoteness from His court.

Behold how the manifold grace of God, which is being showered from the clouds of Divine glory, hath, in this day, encompassed the world. For whereas in days past every lover besought and searched after his Beloved, it is the Beloved Himself Who now is calling His lovers and is inviting them to attain His presence. Take heed lest ye forfeit so precious a favor; beware lest ye belittle so remarkable a token of His grace. Abandon not the incorruptible benefits, and be not content with that which perisheth. Lift up the veil that obscureth your vision, and dispel the darkness with which it is enveloped, that ye may gaze on the naked beauty of the Beloved's face, may behold that which no eye hath beheld, and hear that which no ear hath heard.

Hear Me, ye mortal birds! In the Rose Garden of changeless splendor a Flower hath begun to bloom, compared to which every other flower is but a thorn, and before the brightness of Whose glory the very essence of beauty must pale and wither. Arise, therefore, and, with the whole enthusiasm of your hearts, with all the eagerness of your souls, the full fervor of your will, and the concentrated efforts of your entire being, strive to attain the paradise of His presence, and endeavor to inhale the fragrance of the incorruptible Flower, to breathe the sweet savors of holiness, and to obtain a portion of this perfume of celestial glory. Whoso followeth this counsel will break his chains asunder, will taste the abandonment of enraptured love, will attain unto his heart's desire, and will surrender his soul into the hands of his Beloved. Bursting through his cage, he will, even as the bird of the spirit, wing his flight to his holy and everlasting nest.

18. O My brother! When a true seeker determineth to take the step of search in the path leading unto the knowledge of the Ancient of Days, he must, before all else, cleanse his heart, which is the seat of the revelation of the inner mysteries of God, from the obscuring dust of all acquired knowledge, and the allusions of the embodiments of satanic fancy. He must purge his breast, which is the sanctuary of the abiding love of the Beloved, of every defilement, and sanctify his soul from all that pertaineth to water and clay, from all shadowy and ephemeral attachments. He must so cleanse his heart that no remnant of either love or hate may linger therein, lest that love blindly incline him to error, or that hate repel him away from the truth. Even as thou dost witness in this Day how most of the people, because of such love and hate, are bereft of the immortal Face, have strayed far from the Embodiments of the Divine

21

mysteries, and, shepherdless, are roaming through the wilderness of oblivion and error.

That seeker must, at all times, put his trust in God, must renounce the peoples of the earth, must detach himself from the world of dust, and cleave unto Him Who is the Lord of Lords. He must never seek to exalt himself above any one, must wash away from the tablet of his heart every trace of pride and vain-glory, must cling unto patience and resignation, observe silence and refrain from idle talk. For the tongue is a smoldering fire, and excess of speech a deadly poison. Material fire consumeth the body, whereas the fire of the tongue devoureth both heart and soul. The force of the former lasteth but for a time, whilst the effects of the latter endureth a century.

That seeker should, also, regard backbiting as grievous error, and keep himself aloof from its dominion, inasmuch as backbiting quencheth the light of the heart, and extinguisheth the life of the soul. He should be content with little, and be freed from all inordinate desire. He should treasure the companionship of them that have renounced the world, and regard avoidance of boastful and worldly people a precious benefit. At the dawn of every day he should commune with God, and, with all his soul, persevere in the quest of his Beloved. He should consume every wayward thought with the flame of His loving mention, and, with the swiftness of lightning, pass by all else save Him. He should succor the dispossessed, and never withhold his favor from the destitute. He should show kindness to animals, how much more unto his fellow-man, to him who is endowed with the power of utterance. He should not hesitate to offer up his life for his Beloved, nor allow the censure of the people to turn him away from the Truth. He should not wish for others that which he doth not wish for himself, nor promise that which he doth not fulfil. With all his heart he should avoid fellowship with evil-doers, and pray for the remission of their sins. He should forgive the sinful, and never despise his low estate, for none knoweth what his own end shall be. How often hath a sinner attained, at the hour of death, to the essence of faith, and, quaffing the immortal draught, hath taken his flight unto the Concourse on high! And how often hath a devout believer, at the hour of his soul's ascension, been so changed as to fall into the nethermost fire!

Our purpose in revealing these convincing and weighty utterances is to impress upon the seeker that he should regard all else beside God as transient, and count all things save Him, Who is the Object of all adoration, as utter nothingness.

These are among the attributes of the exalted, and constitute the hall-mark of the spiritually-minded. They have already been mentioned in connection with the requirements of the wayfarers that tread the path of Positive Knowledge. When the detached wayfarer and sincere seeker hath fulfilled these essential conditions, then and only then can he be called a true seeker. Whensoever he hath fulfilled the conditions implied in the verse: "Whoso maketh efforts for Us," he shall enjoy the blessings conferred by the words: "In Our Ways shall We assuredly guide him."

Only when the lamp of search, of earnest striving, of longing desire, of passionate devotion, of fervid love, of rapture, and ecstasy, is kindled within the seeker's heart, and the breeze of His loving-kindness is wafted upon his soul, will the darkness of error be dispelled, the mists of doubts and misgivings be dissipated, and the lights of knowledge and certitude envelop his being. At that hour will the Mystic Herald, bearing the joyful tidings of the Spirit, shine forth from the City of God resplendent as the morn, and, through the trumpet-blast of knowledge, will awaken the heart, the soul, and the spirit from the slumber of heedlessness. Then will the manifold favors and out-pouring grace of the holy and everlasting Spirit confer such new life upon the seeker that he will find himself endowed with a new eye, a new ear, a new heart, and a new mind. He will contemplate the manifest signs of the universe, and will penetrate the hidden mysteries of the soul. Gazing with the eye of God, he will perceive within every atom a door that leadeth him to the stations of abso-lute certitude. He will discover in all things the mysteries of Divine Revelation, and the evidences of an everlasting Manifestation. . . .

When the channel of the human soul is cleansed of all worldly and impeding attachments, it will unfailingly per-ceive the breath of the Beloved across immeasurable dis-tances, and will, led by its perfume, attain and enter the City of Certitude. . . .

They that valiantly labor in quest of God, will, when once they have renounced all else but Him, be so attached and wedded unto that City, that a moment's separation from it would to them be unthinkable. They will hearken unto infallible proofs from the Hyacinth of that assembly, and will receive the surest testimonies from the beauty of its Rose, and the melody of its Nightingale. Once in about a thousand years shall this City be renewed and readorned.

That City is none other than the Word of God revealed in every age and dispensation. In the days of Moses it was the Pentateuch; in the days of Jesus, the Gospel; in the days of Muḥammad, the Messenger of God, the Qur'án; in this day, the Bayán; and in the Dispensation of Him Whom God will make manifest, His own Book—the Book unto which all the Books of former Dispensations must needs be referred, the Book that standeth amongst them all transcendent and supreme.

19. Be generous in prosperity, and thankful in adversity.
Be worthy of the trust of thy neighbor, and look upon him
with a bright and friendly face. Be a treasure to the poor,
an admonisher to the rich, an answerer of the cry of the
needy, a preserver of the sanctity of thy pledge. Be fair
in thy judgment, and guarded in thy speech. Be unjust
to no man, and show all meekness to all men. Be as a
lamp unto them that walk in darkness, a joy to the sorrow-
ful, a sea for the thirsty, a haven for the distressed, an
upholder and defender of the victim of oppression. Let
integrity and uprightness distinguish all thine acts. Be
a home for the stranger, a balm to the suffering, a tower
of strength for the fugitive. Be eyes to the blind, and a
guiding light unto the feet of the erring. Be an ornament
to the countenance of truth, a crown to the brow of fidelity,
a pillar of the temple of righteousness, a breath of life to
the body of mankind, an ensign of the hosts of justice, a
luminary above the horizon of virtue, a dew to the soil of
the human heart, an ark on the ocean of knowledge, a
sun in the heaven of bounty, a gem on the diadem of wisdom, a shining light in the firmament of thy generation, a
fruit upon the tree of humility.

20. Beautify your tongues, O people, with truthfulness, and
adorn your souls with the ornament of honesty. Beware,
O people, that ye deal not treacherously with any one. Be
ye the trustees of God amongst His creatures, and the em-
blems of His generosity amidst His people. They that
follow their lusts and corrupt inclinations, have erred and
dissipated their efforts. They, indeed, are of the lost.
Strive, O people, that your eyes may be directed towards
the mercy of God, that your hearts may be attuned to His
wondrous remembrance, that your souls may rest confident-
ly upon His grace and bounty, that your feet may tread

the path of His good-pleasure. Such are the counsels which I bequeath unto you. Would that ye might follow My counsels!

21. Gird up the loins of thine endeavor, that haply thou mayest guide thy neighbor to the law of God, the Most Merciful. Such an act, verily, excelleth all other acts in the sight of God, the All-Possessing, the Most High. Such must be thy steadfastness in the Cause of God, that no earthly thing whatsoever will have the power to deter thee from thy duty. Though the powers of earth be leagued against thee, though all men dispute with thee, thou must remain unshaken.

Be unrestrained as the wind, while carrying the Message of Him Who hath caused the Dawn of Divine Guidance to break. Consider, how the wind, faithful to that which God hath ordained, bloweth upon all the regions of the earth, be they inhabited or desolate. Neither the sight of desolation, nor the evidences of prosperity, can either pain or please it. It bloweth in every direction, as bidden by its Creator. So should be every one that claimeth to be a lover of the one true God. It behoveth him to fix his gaze upon the fundamentals of His Faith, and to labor diligently for its propagation. Wholly for the sake of God he should proclaim His Message, and with that same spirit accept whatever response his words may evoke in his hearer. He who shall accept and believe, shall receive his reward; and he who shall turn away, shall receive none other than his own punishment.

22. Do thou beseech God to enable thee to remain steadfast in this path, and to aid thee to guide the peoples of the world to Him Who is the manifest and sovereign Ruler, Who hath revealed Himself in a distinct attire, Who giveth

utterance to a Divine and specific Message. This is the essence of faith and certitude. They that are the worshipers of the idol which their imaginations have carved, and who call it Inner Reality, such men are in truth accounted among the heathen. To this hath the All-Merciful borne witness in His Tablets. He, verily, is the All-Knowing, the All-Wise.

23. The ordinances of God have been sent down from the heaven of His most august Revelation. All must diligently observe them. Man's supreme distinction, his real advancement, his final victory, have always depended, and will continue to depend, upon them. Whoso keepeth the commandments of God shall attain everlasting felicity.

A twofold obligation resteth upon him who hath recognized the Day Spring of the Unity of God, and acknowledged the truth of Him Who is the Manifestation of His oneness. The first is steadfastness in His love, such steadfastness that neither the clamor of the enemy nor the claims of the idle pretender can deter him from cleaving unto Him Who is the Enternal Truth, a steadfastness that taketh no account of them whatever. The second is strict observance of the laws He hath prescribed—laws which He hath always ordained, and will continue to ordain, unto men, and through which the truth may be distinguished and separated from falsehood.

24. By My Beauty! Nothing whatsoever shall, in this Day, be accepted from you, though ye continue to worship and prostrate yourselves before God throughout the eternity of His dominion. For all things are dependent upon His Will, and the worth of all acts is conditioned upon His acceptance and pleasure. The whole universe is but a handful of clay in His grasp. Unless one recognizes God

and loves Him, his cry shall not be heard by God in this Day. This is of the essence of His Faith, did ye but know it.

25. Know assuredly that just as thou firmly believest that the Word of God, exalted be His glory, endureth for ever, thou must, likewise, believe with undoubting faith that its meaning can never be exhausted. They who are its appointed interpreters, they whose hearts are the repositories of its secrets, are, however, the only ones who can comprehend its manifold wisdom. Whoso, while reading the Sacred Scriptures, is tempted to choose therefrom whatever may suit him with which to challenge the authority of the Representative of God among men, is indeed, as one dead, though to outward seeming he may walk and converse with his neighbors, and share with them their food and their drink. . . .

We beseech God to strengthen thee with His power, and enable thee to recognize Him Who is the Source of all knowledge, that thou mayest detach thyself from all human learning, for, "what would it profit any man to strive after learning when he hath already found and recognized Him Who is the Object of all knowledge?" Cleave to the Root of Knowledge, and to Him Who is the Fountain thereof, that thou mayest find thyself independent of all who claim to be well versed in human learning, and whose claim no clear proof, nor the testimony of any enlightening book, can support.

26. O My servants! Sorrow not if, in these days and on this earthly plane, things contrary to your wishes have been ordained and manifested by God, for days of blissful joy, of heavenly delight, are assuredly in store for you. Worlds, holy and spiritually glorious, will be unveiled to

28

your eyes. You are destined by Him, in this world and hereafter, to partake of their benefits, to share in their joys, and to obtain a portion of their sustaining grace. To each and every one of them you will, no doubt, attain.

27. Know thou for a certainty that whoso disbelieveth in God is neither trustworthy nor truthful. This, indeed, is the truth, the undoubted truth. He that acteth treacherously towards God will, also, act treacherously towards his king. Nothing whatever can deter such a man from evil, nothing can hinder him from betraying his neighbor, nothing can induce him to walk uprightly.

28. Intone, O My servant, the verses of God that have been received by thee, as intoned by them who have drawn nigh unto Him, that the sweetness of thy melody may kindle thine own soul, and attract the hearts of all men. Whoso reciteth, in the privacy of his chamber, the verses revealed by God, the scattering angels of the Almighty shall scatter abroad the fragrance of the words uttered by his mouth, and shall cause the heart of every righteous man to throb.

Progress of the Soul

29. Know thou of a truth that the soul, after its separation from the body, will continue to progress until it attaineth the presence of God, in a state and condition which neither the revolution of ages and centuries, nor the changes and chances of this world, can alter. It will endure as long as the Kingdom of God, His sovereignty, His dominion and power will endure. It will manifest the signs of God and His attributes, and will reveal His loving kindness and bounty. The movement of My Pen is stilled when it attempteth to befittingly describe the loftiness and glory

of so exalted a station. The honor with which the Hand of Mercy will invest the soul is such as no tongue can adequately reveal, nor any other earthly agency describe. Blessed is the soul which, at the hour of its separation from the body, is sanctified from the vain imaginings of the peoples of the world. Such a soul liveth and moveth in accordance with the Will of its Creator, and entereth the all-highest Paradise.

30. And now concerning thy question whether human souls continue to be conscious one of another after their separation from the body. Know thou that the souls of the people of Bahá, who have entered and been established within the Crimson Ark, shall associate and commune intimately one with another, and shall be so closely associated in their lives, their aspirations, their aims and strivings as to be even as one soul. They are indeed the ones who are well-informed, who are keen-sighted, and who are endued with understanding. Thus hath it been decreed by Him Who is the All-Knowing, the All-Wise.

31. Know thou that all men have been created in the nature made by God, the Guardian, the Self-Subsisting. Unto each one hath been prescribed a pre-ordained measure, as decreed in God's mighty and guarded Tablets. All that which ye potentially possess can, however, be manifested only as a result of your own volition.

32. Know thou that the soul of man is exalted above, and is independent of all infirmities of body or mind. That a sick person showeth signs of weakness is due to the hindrances that interpose themselves between his soul and his body, for the soul itself remaineth unaffected by any bodily ailments. Consider the light of the lamp. Though an

external object may interfere with its radiance, the light itself continueth to shine with undiminished power. In like manner, every malady afflicting the body of man is an impediment that preventeth the soul from manifesting its inherent might and power. When it leaveth the body, however, it will evince such ascendancy, and reveal such influence as no force on earth can equal. Every pure, every refined and sanctified soul will be endowed with tremendous power, and shall rejoice with exceeding gladness.

Attainment of Peace and Tranquillity

33. The world is in travail, and its agitation waxeth day by day. Its face is turned towards waywardness and unbelief. Such shall be its plight, that to disclose it now would not be meet and seemly. Its perversity will long continue. And when the appointed hour is come, there shall suddenly appear that which shall cause the limbs of mankind to quake. Then, and only then, will the Divine Standard be unfurled, and the Nightingale of Paradise warble its melody.

34. The utterance of God is a lamp, whose light is these words: Ye are the fruits of one tree, and the leaves of one branch. Deal ye one with another with the utmost love and harmony, with friendliness and fellowship. He Who is the Day Star of Truth beareth Me witness! So powerful is the light of unity that it can illuminate the whole earth. The one true God, He Who knoweth all things, Himself testifieth to the truth of these words.

Exert yourselves that ye may attain this transcendent and most sublime station, the station that can insure the protection and security of all mankind. This goal excelleth every other goal, and this aspiration is the monarch of all aspirations. So long, however, as the thick clouds of oppression, which obscure the day star of justice, remain undispelled, it would be difficult for the glory of this station to be unveiled to men's eyes. . . .

35. O contending peoples and kindreds of the earth! Set your faces towards unity, and let the radiance of its light shine upon you. Gather ye together, and for the sake of God resolve to root out whatever is the source of contention amongst you. Then will the effulgence of the world's great Luminary envelop the whole earth, and its inhabitants become the citizens of one city, and the occupants of one and the same throne. This wronged One hath, ever since the early days of His life, cherished none other desire but this, and will continue to entertain no wish except this wish. There can be no doubt whatever that the peoples of the world, of whatever race or religion, derive their inspiration from one heavenly Source, and are the subjects of one God. The difference between the ordinances under which they abide should be attributed to the varying requirements and exigencies of the age in which they were revealed. All of them, except a few which are the outcome of human perversity, were ordained of God, and are a reflection of His Will and Purpose. Arise and, armed with the power of faith, shatter to pieces the gods of your vain imaginings, the sowers of dissension amongst you. Cleave unto that which draweth you together and uniteth you.

36. The Great Being, wishing to reveal the prerequisites of the peace and tranquillity of the world and the advancement of its peoples, hath written: The time must come when the imperative necessity for the holding of a vast, an all-embracing assemblage of men will be universally realized. The rulers and kings of the earth must needs attend it, and,

participating in its deliberations, must consider such ways and means as will lay the foundations of the world's Great Peace amongst men. Such a peace demandeth that the Great Powers should resolve, for the sake of the tranquillity of the peoples of the earth, to be fully reconciled among themselves. Should any king take up arms against another, all should unitedly arise and prevent him. If this be done, the nations of the world will no longer require any armaments, except for the purpose of preserving the security of their realms and of maintaining internal order within their territories. This will insure the peace and composure of every people, government and nation.

37. Now that ye have refused the Most Great Peace, hold ye fast unto this, the Lesser Peace, that haply ye may in some degree better your own condition and that of your dependents.

O rulers of the earth! Be reconciled among yourselves, that ye may need no more armaments save in a measure to safeguard your territories and dominions. Beware lest ye disregard the counsel of the All-Knowing, the Faithful.

Be united, O kings of the earth, for thereby will the tempest of discord be stilled amongst you, and your peoples find rest, if ye be of them that comprehend. Should any one among you take up arms against another, rise ye all against him, for this is naught but manifest justice.

38. O ye the elected representatives of the people in every land! Take ye counsel together, and let your concern be only for that which profiteth mankind, and bettereth the condition thereof, if ye be of them that scan heedfully. Regard the world as the human body which, though at its creation whole and perfect, hath been afflicted, through various causes, with grave disorders and maladies. Not

for one day did it gain ease, nay its sickness waxed more severe, as it fell under the treatment of ignorant physicians, who gave full rein to their personal desires, and have erred grievously. And if, at one time, through the care of an able physician, a member of that body was healed, the rest remained afflicted as before. Thus informeth you the All-Knowing, the All-Wise.

We behold it, in this day, at the mercy of rulers so drunk with pride that they cannot discern clearly their own best advantage, much less recognize a Revelation so bewildering and challenging as this. And whenever any one of them hath striven to improve its condition, his motive hath been his own gain, whether confessedly so or not; and the unworthiness of this motive hath limited his power to heal or cure.

That which the Lord hath ordained as the sovereign remedy and mightiest instrument for the healing of all the world is the union of all its peoples in one universal Cause, one common Faith. This can in no wise be achieved except through the power of a skilled, an all-powerful and inspired Physician. This, verily, is the truth, and all else naught but error.

39. All men have been created to carry forward an ever-advancing civilization. The Almighty beareth Me witness: To act like the beasts of the field is unworthy of man. Those virtues that befit his dignity are forbearance, mercy, compassion and loving-kindness towards all the peoples and kindreds of the earth. Say: O friends! Drink your fill from this crystal stream that floweth through the heavenly grace of Him Who is the Lord of Names. Let others partake of its waters in My name, that the leaders of men in every land may fully recognize the purpose for which the

Eternal Truth hath been revealed, and the reason for which they themselves have been created.

40. The All-Knowing Physician hath His finger on the pulse of mankind. He perceiveth the disease, and prescribeth, in His unerring wisdom, the remedy. Every age hath its own problem, and every soul its particular aspiration. The remedy the world needeth in its present-day afflictions can never be the same as that which a subsequent age may require. Be anxiously concerned with the needs of the age ye live in, and center your deliberations on its exigencies and requirements.

We can well perceive how the whole human race is encompassed with great, with incalculable afflictions. We see it languishing on its bed of sickness, sore-tried and disillusioned. They that are intoxicated by self-conceit have interposed themselves between it and the Divine and infallible Physician. Witness how they have entangled all men, themselves included, in the mesh of their devices. They can neither discover the cause of the disease, nor have they any knowledge of the remedy. They have conceived the straight to be crooked, and have imagined their friend an enemy.

41. How vast is the tabernacle of the Cause of God! It hath overshadowed all the peoples and kindreds of the earth, and will, erelong, gather together the whole of mankind beneath its shelter. Thy day of service is now come. Countless Tablets bear the testimony of the bounties vouchsafed unto thee. Arise for the triumph of My Cause, and, through the power of thine utterance, subdue the hearts of men. Thou must show forth that which will insure the peace and the well-being of the miserable and the downtrodden. Gird up the loins of thine endeavor, that per-

chance thou mayest release the captive from his chains, and enable him to attain unto true liberty.

Justice is, in this day, bewailing its plight, and Equity groaneth beneath the yoke of oppression. The thick clouds of tyranny have darkened the face of the earth, and enveloped its peoples. Through the movement of Our Pen of glory We have, at the bidding of the omnipotent Ordainer, breathed a new life into every human frame, and instilled into every word a fresh potency. All created things proclaim the evidences of this world-wide regeneration. This is the most great, the most joyful tidings imparted by the pen of this wronged One to mankind. Wherefore fear ye, O My well-beloved ones! Who is it that can dismay you? A touch of moisture sufficeth to dissolve the hardened clay out of which this perverse generation is molded. The mere act of your gathering together is enough to scatter the forces of these vain and worthless people. . . .

Every man of insight will, in this day, readily admit that the counsels which the Pen of this wronged One hath revealed constitute the supreme animating power for the advancement of the world and the exaltation of its peoples. Arise, O people, and, by the power of God's might, resolve to gain the victory over your own selves, that haply the whole earth may be freed and sancified from its servitude to the gods of its idle fancies—gods that have inflicted such loss upon, and are responsible for the misery of, their wretched worshipers. These idols form the obstacle that impeded man in his efforts to advance in the path of perfection. We cherish the hope that the Hand of Divine power may lend its assistance to mankind, and deliver it from its state of grievous abasement.

In one of the Tablets these words have been revealed: O people of God! Do not busy yourselves in your own concerns; let your thoughts be fixed upon that which will rehabilitate the fortunes of mankind and sanctify the hearts and souls of men. This can best be achieved through pure and holy deeds, through a virtuous life and a goodly behavior. Valiant acts will insure the triumph of this Cause, and a saintly character will reinforce its power. Cleave unto righteousness, O people of Bahá! This, verily, is the commandment which this wronged One hath given unto you, and the first choice of His unrestrained Will for every one of you.

O friends! It behoveth you to refresh and revive your souls through the gracious favors which in this Divine, this soul-stirring Springtime are being showered upon you. The Day Star of His great glory hath shed its radiance upon you, and the clouds of His limitless grace have overshadowed you. How high the reward of him that hath not deprived himself of so great a bounty, nor failed to recognize the beauty of his Best-Beloved in this, His new attire. Watch over yourselves, for the Evil One is lying in wait, ready to entrap you. Gird yourselves against his wicked devices, and, led by the light of the name of the All-Seeing God, make your escape from the darkness that surroundeth you. Let your vision be world-embracing, rather than confined to your own self. The Evil One is he that hindereth the rise and obstructeth the spiritual progress of the children of men.

It is incumbent upon every man, in this Day, to hold fast unto whatsoever will promote the interests, and exalt the station, of all nations and just governments. Through each and every one of the verses which the Pen of the Most High hath revealed, the doors of love and unity have been unlocked and flung open to the face of men. We have erewhile declared—and Our Word is the truth—: "Consort with the followers of all religions in a spirit of friendliness and fellowship." Whatsoever hath led the children of men to shun one another, and hath caused dissensions and divisions amongst them, hath, through the revelation of these words, been nullified and abolished. From the heaven of God's Will, and for the purpose of ennobling the world of being and of elevating the minds and souls of men, hath been sent down that which is the most effective instrument for the education of the whole human race. The highest essence and most perfect expression of whatsoever the peoples of old have either said or written hath, through this most potent Revelation, been sent down from the heaven of the Will of the All-Possessing, the Ever-Abiding God. Of old it hath been revealed: "Love of one's country is an element of the Faith of God." The Tongue of Grandeur hath, however, in the day of His manifestation proclaimed: "It is not his to boast who loveth his country, but it is his who loveth the world." Through the power released by these exalted words He hath lent a fresh impulse, and set a new direction, to the birds of men's hearts, and hath obliterated every trace of restriction and limitation from God's holy Book.

O people of Justice! Be as brilliant as the light, and as splendid as the fire that blazed in the Burning Bush. The brightness of the fire of your love will no doubt fuse and unify the contending peoples and kindreds of the earth, whilst the fierceness of the flame of enmity and hatred cannot but result in strife and ruin. We beseech God that He may shield His creatures from the evil designs of His enemies. He verily hath power over all things.

All-praise be to the one true God—exalted be His glory —inasmuch as He hath, through the Pen of the Most High, unlocked the doors of men's hearts. Every verse which this Pen hath revealed is a bright and shining portal that discloseth the glories of a saintly and pious life, of pure and stainless deeds. The summons and the message which

We gave were never intended to reach or to benefit one land or one people only. Mankind in its entirety must firmly adhere to whatsoever hath been revealed and vouchsafed unto it. Then and only then will it attain unto true liberty. The whole earth is illuminated with the resplendent glory of God's Revelation.

42. The One true God beareth Me witness, and His creatures will testify, that not for a moment did I allow Myself to be hidden from the eyes of men, nor did I consent to shield My person from their injury. Before the face of all men I have arisen, and bidden them fulfil My pleasure. My object is none other than the betterment of the world and the tranquillity of its peoples. The well-being of mankind, its peace and security, are unattainable unless and until its unity is firmly established. This unity can never be achieved so long as the counsels which the Pen of the Most High hath revealed are suffered to pass unheeded.

Through the power of the words He hath uttered the whole of the human race can be illumined with the light of unity, and the remembrance of His Name is able to set on fire the hearts of all men, and burn away the veils that intervene between them and His glory. One righteous act is endowed with a potency that can so elevate the dust as to cause it to pass beyond the heaven of heavens. It can tear every bond asunder, and hath the power to restore the force that hath spent itself and vanished. . . .

43. The purpose of the one true God, exalted be His Glory, in revealing Himself unto men is to lay bare those gems that lie hidden within the mine of their true and inmost selves. That the divers communions of the earth, and the manifold systems of religious belief, should never be allowed to foster the feelings of animosity among men, is,

in this Day, of the essence of the Faith of God and His Religion. These principles and laws, these firmly-established and mighty systems, have proceeded from one Source, and are the rays of one Light. That they differ one from another is to be attributed to the varying requirements of the ages in which they were promulgated.

Gird up the loins of your endeavor, O people of Bahá, that haply the tumult of religious dissension and strife that agitateth the peoples of the earth may be stilled, that every trace of it may be completely obliterated. For the love of God, and them that serve Him, arise to aid this most sublime and momentous Revelation. Religious fanaticism and hatred are a world-devouring fire, whose violence none can quench. The Hand of Divine power can, alone, deliver mankind from this desolating affliction.

44. The affairs of the people are placed in charge of the men of the House of Justice of God. They are the trustees of God among His servants and the day springs of command in His countries.

O people of God! The trainer of the world is Justice, for it consisteth of two pillars: Reward and Retribution. These two pillars are two fountains for the life of the people of the world. Inasmuch as for each time and day a particular decree and order is expedient, affairs are therefore entrusted to the ministers of the House of Justice, so that they may execute that which they deem advisable at the time. Those souls who arise to serve the Cause sincerely to please God will be inspired by the divine, invisible inspirations. It is incumbent upon all to obey.

Administrative affairs are all in charge of the House of Justice; but acts of worship must be observed according as they are revealed in the Book. . . . The ministers of the House of Justice must promote the Most Great Peace, in order that the world may be freed from onerous expenditure. This matter is obligatory and indispensable; for warfare and conflict are the foundation of trouble and distress.

45. Whoso layeth claim to a Revelation direct from God, ere the expiration of a full thousand years, such a man is assuredly a lying impostor. We pray God that He may graciously assist him to retract and repudiate such claim. Should he repent, God will, no doubt, forgive him. If, however, he persisteth in his error, God will, assuredly, send down one who will deal mercilessly with him. Terrible, indeed, is God in punishing! Whosoever interpreteth this verse otherwise than its obvious meaning is deprived of the Spirit of God and of His mercy which encompasseth all created things. Fear God, and follow not your idle fancies. Nay, rather follow the bidding of your Lord, the Almighty, the All-Wise.

The Covenant Thou Hast Established

46. Glorified art Thou, O my God! Thou knowest that my sole aim in revealing Thy Cause hath been to reveal Thee and not myself, and to manifest Thy glory rather than my glory. In Thy path, and to attain Thy pleasure, I have scorned rest, joy, delight. At all times and under all conditions my gaze hath been fixed on Thy precepts, and mine eyes bent upon the things Thou hast bidden me observe in Thy Tablets. I have wakened every morning to the light of Thy praise and Thy remembrance, and reached every evening inhaling the fragrances of Thy mercy.

And when the entire creation was stirred up, and the whole earth was convulsed, and the sweet savors of Thy name, the All-Praised, had almost ceased to breathe over Thy realms, and the winds of Thy mercy had well-nigh been stilled throughout Thy dominions, Thou didst, through the power of Thy might, raise me up among Thy servants, and bid me to show forth Thy sovereignty amidst Thy people. Therefore I arose before all Thy creatures, strengthened by Thy help and Thy power, and summoned all the multitudes unto Thee, and announced unto all Thy servants Thy favors and Thy gifts, and invited them to turn towards this Ocean, every drop of the waters of which crieth out, proclaiming unto all that are in heaven and on earth that He is, in truth, the Fountain of all life, and the Quickener of the entire creation, and the Object of the adoration of all worlds, and the Best-Beloved of every understanding heart, and the Desire of all them that are nigh unto Thee.

Though the fierce winds of the hatred of the wicked doers blew and beat on this Lamp, He was, at no time, in His love for Thy beauty, hindered from shedding the fragrance of His light. As the transgressions committed against Thee waxed greater and greater, my eagerness to reveal Thy Cause correspondingly increased, and as the tribulations deepened—and to this Thy glory beareth me witness—a fuller measure of Thy sovereignty and of Thy power was vouchsafed by me unto Thy creatures.

And finally, I was cast by the transgressors into the prison-city of 'Akká, and my kindred were made captives in Baghdád. The power of Thy might beareth me witness, O my God! Every trouble that hath touched me in Thy path hath added to my joy and increased my gladness. I swear by Thee, O Thou Who art the King of Kings! None of the kings of the earth hath power to hinder me from remembering Thee or from extolling Thy virtues. Were they to be leagued—as they have been leagued—against me, and to brandish their sharpest swords and most afflictive spears against me, I would not hesitate to magnify Thy name before all them that are in Thy heaven and on Thy earth. Nay rather, I would cry out and say: "This, O my Beloved, is my face which I have offered up for Thy face, and this is my spirit which I have sacrificed for Thy spirit, and this is my blood that seetheth in my veins, in its longing to be shed for love of Thee and in Thy path."

Though—as Thou beholdest me, O my God—I be dwelling in a place within whose walls no voice can be heard except the sound of the echo, though all the gates of ease and comfort be shut against us, and thick darkness appear to have encompassed us on every side, yet my soul hath been so inflamed by its love for Thee, that nothing whatever can either quench the fire of its love or abate the consuming flame of its desire. Lifting up its voice, it crieth aloud amidst Thy servants, and calleth them, at all times and under all conditions, unto Thee.

I beseech Thee, by Thy Most Great Name, to open the eyes of Thy servants, that they may behold Thee shining above the horizon of Thy majesty and glory, and that they may not be hindered by the croaking of the raven from hearkening to the voice of the Dove of Thy sublime oneness, nor be prevented by the corrupt waters from partaking of the pure wine of Thy bounty and the everlasting streams of Thy gifts.

Gather them, then, together around this Divine Law, the covenant of which Thou hast established with all Thy prophets and Thy messengers, and Whose ordinances Thou hast written down in Thy Tablets and Thy Scriptures, raise them up, moreover, to such heights as will enable them to perceive Thy call.

Potent art Thou to do what pleaseth Thee. Thou art, verily, the Inaccessible, the All-Glorious.